Cultural Traditions

Brazil

Molly
Aloian

Crabtree Publishing Company

www.crabtreebooks.com

Crabtree Publishing Company

www.crabtreebooks.com

Author: Molly Aloian
Publishing plan research and development:
   Sean Charlebois, Reagan Miller
   Crabtree Publishing Company
Project coordinator: Kathy Middleton
Editor: Crystal Sikkens
Proofreader: Kathy Middleton
Photo research: Allison Napier, Crystal Sikkens
Design: Margaret Amy Salter
Production coordinator: Margaret Amy Salter
Prepress technician: Margaret Amy Salter
Print coordinator: Katherine Berti

Cover: Christ the Redeemer statue in Rio de Janeiro (top); woman at carnival (middle center); cathedral of Brasilia (middle right); statue of Yemanja, the queen of the sea (middle left); art showing our Lady of the Aparecida (bottom center); Brazilian traditional dish called *feijoada* (bottom left)

Title page: A male samba dancer at carnival in Rio de Janerio

Photographs:
Alamy: © Peter M. Wilson: page 12; Prisma Archivo: page 31 (bottom)
Associated Press: Alexandre Meneghini: page 18
Dreamstime: Ducalazans: page 19 (top)
Keystone Press: Charles Silva Duarte/zumapress.com: page 16; Tarso Sarraf/zumapress: page 29
Shutterstock: ostill: front cover (top); Alexander Bark: front cover (bottom center), page 21 (bottom left); gary yim: front cover (middle right), pages 1, 10, 11; pixshots: front cover (bottom left); Mark William Penny: front cover (middle center); Vinicius Tupinamba: front cover (middle left), page 13 (middle); Marc Turcan: page 4; Mark Schwettmann: page 5; marvellousworld: page 7 (top); Luciana Bueno: page 13 (top); Celso Pupo: page 22 (right)
Thinkstock: iStockphoto: page 8; Hemera: page 19 (bottom)
Wikimedia Commons: Eduardo P: page 6; André Koehne: page 7 (bottom); Fabio Rodrigues Pozzebom/ABr: pages 9, 25; João Medeiros: page 13 (bottom); Valter Campanato/ABr: pages 14, 15, 23, 26; Andrevruas: pages 17, 28; Filipux: page 20; Bruno Coitinho Araújo: page 21 (top); David Cardoso: page 21 (bottom right); Carneiro & Gaspar: page 22 (left); Wilson Dias/ABr: page 24 (top); Victor Soares/ABr: page 24 (bottom); Eugenio Hansen, OFS: page 27 (top); HVL: page 27 (bottom); Delfim da Câmara/Museu Histórico Nacional (MHN): page 30; Alex Pereira: page 31 (top)

Library and Archives Canada Cataloguing in Publication

Aloian, Molly
   Cultural traditions in Brazil / Molly Aloian.

(Cultural traditions in my world)
Includes index.
Issued also in electronic format.
ISBN 978-0-7787-7583-6 (bound).--ISBN 978-0-7787-7590-4 (pbk.)

   1. Festivals--Brazil--Juvenile literature. 2. Holidays--Brazil--Juvenile literature. 3. Brazil--Social life and customs--Juvenile literature. I. Title. II. Series: Cultural traditions in my world

GT4833.A2A56 2012   j394.26981   C2012-900863-X

Library of Congress Cataloging-in-Publication Data

Aloian, Molly.
Cultural traditions in Brazil / Molly Aloian.
p. cm. -- (Cultural traditions in my world)
Includes index.
ISBN 978-0-7787-7583-6 (reinforced library binding : alk. paper) --
ISBN 978-0-7787-7590-4 (pbk. : alk. paper) -- ISBN 978-1-4271-7862-6
(electronic pdf) -- ISBN 978-1-4271-7977-7 (electronic html)
1. Holidays--Brazil--Juvenile literature. 2. Festivals--Brazil--Juvenile literature.
3. Brazil--Social life and customs--Juvenile literature. I. Title.

GT4833.A2A67 2012
394.26981--dc23
                                    2012004028

Crabtree Publishing Company

www.crabtreebooks.com   1-800-387-7650
Printed in the U.S.A./032012/CJ20120215

Published in Canada
Crabtree Publishing
616 Welland Ave.
St. Catharines, ON
L2M 5V6

Published in the United States
Crabtree Publishing
PMB 59051
350 Fifth Avenue, 59th Floor
New York, New York 10118

Published in the United Kingdom
Crabtree Publishing
Maritime House
Basin Road North, Hove
BN41 1WR

Published in Australia
Crabtree Publishing
3 Charles Street
Coburg North
VIC 3058

Contents

Welcome to Brazil

Brazil is the largest country in South America, both in size and population. Over 200 million people live in Brazil and most people speak Portuguese. Brazil lies primarily to the east of South America and borders the Atlantic Ocean. Most of Brazil has a tropical climate with a variety of landscapes including rainforests, wetlands, savannas, mountains, and plateaus.

Did You Know?
Brazil's capital city is Brasilia. Over 2.5 million people live in Brasilia.

Brazil has 4,600 miles (7,400 km) of coastline with many beautiful beaches.

Cultural traditions are the holidays, festivals, traditions, and customs that groups of people celebrate each year. Some cultural traditions are religious celebrations. Others celebrate an important day in history or personal events such as birthdays and weddings. This book highlights the cultural traditions in the country of Brazil.

The majority of Brazilians follow the Roman Catholic Church and believe Jesus Christ is the son of God and their Lord and Savior. To honor Him, an enormous statue was completed in 1931 on Mount Corcovado, in Rio de Janeiro.

Christmas

Many people in Brazil celebrate Christmas on December 25 each year. Families gather together to decorate Christmas trees and share a big supper on Christmas Eve or Christmas Day. People enjoy Christmas foods such as roast duck or roast pig, turkey, baked ham, vegetables, fresh fruit, and nuts. Many people also set up **nativity scenes** in or around their homes. In Brazil, a nativity scene is called a Presépio.

Some people create large nativity scenes like this one in Governador Valadares, Brazil.

In Brazil, Santa Claus is called Papai Noel. A tradition on Christmas Eve is for children to leave their shoes near an open window so that Papai Noel will fill them with presents. On Christmas morning, children also search for gifts left by Papai Noel that are hidden around the house.

In December, it is hot and sunny in most of Brazil. Some people celebrate Christmas on the beach.

Children can visit Papai Noel at many malls in Brazilian cities.

New Year's Eve

New Year's Eve is one of the most celebrated holidays in Brazil. As in most places around the world, Brazilians celebrate New Year's Eve on December 31 each year. Millions of people gather for large parties on beaches. There is music and dancing, and a spectacular fireworks show set off at midnight.

Copacabana Beach hosts a big New Year's celebration each year.

Many people also come to the beach on New Year's Eve to celebrate the Festa de Iemanjá. In Brazil, many people believe Iemanjá is the Goddess of the Water. People offer Iemanjá flowers, perfume, rice, and other gifts. People set these items into little boats and place them into the water or toss the items directly into the water. The gifts are offered as thanks for the past year and for the year to come.

Did You Know?
Different places throughout Brazil honor Iemanjá with flowers and gifts at different times of the year. Some honor her on New Year's Eve, others give thanks to her on December 8 or February 2.

Carnival

People in cities, towns, and villages throughout Brazil celebrate carnival in February or March. It is a four-day celebration that takes place 40 days before Easter. People wear beautiful costumes, sing, dance, and share food as a way to celebrate and have fun before Lent, a religious holiday during which people **fast**.

Did You Know?
Most Brazilian offices and businesses close for the entire week during carnival.

Parades are a big part of carnival. Many have large, colorful floats, especially the famous parade in Rio de Janeiro.

People in Brazil have celebrated carnival for hundreds of years. This celebration is a very important part of Brazilian culture. The biggest and most well-known carnival celebration takes place in Rio de Janeiro. One of the highlights of carnival in Rio de Janeiro is the long, colorful parade of the top samba schools. Samba is a Brazilian dance.

Samba dancers are dressed in beautiful costumes in all different colors.

11

Easter

Many Easter traditions in Brazil are similar to those of other Catholic countries. Easter takes place after carnival and commemorates the **resurrection** of Jesus Christ. Holy Week, or the week before Easter, is observed throughout the country. **Procession** walks take place and people go to church to attend Mass. Many people carry palm branches that are blessed at church and taken home.

In the city of Ouro Preto, Brazil, a colorful carpet made of sawdust and rice husks is created for the processional walk on Easter Sunday.

Giving and receiving chocolate eggs is a favorite Easter tradition in Brazil. Chocolate eggs are often wrapped in colorful foil and filled with other chocolates and goodies. Easter ring cake and salt cod are other foods enjoyed by Brazilians at Easter.

People use salt cod to make salt cod balls called *bolinho de bacalhau* in Portuguese.

Did You Know?
The Macela flower only blooms during the Lent season. Some people use it in herbal medicines and believe it will cure certain illnesses.

Indian Day

Brazilian Indian Day takes place on April 19 each year. On this day, people learn about and celebrate Brazilian **indigenous** peoples. It is one of the largest indigenous cultural events in the world. Some of the National Indigenous Festival's main attractions include indigenous rituals, body art, music, dance, food, crafts, and sports.

Face and body painting are popular activities on Brazilian Indian Day.

Each year, new ethnic groups are invited to the festival. Over 450,000 people from 225 different societies live in indigenous villages called aldeias in Brazil. They speak more than 180 distinct languages. An estimated 100,000 to 190,000 Brazilian Indians live outside the aldeias, and some small groups in remote areas are still isolated.

Did You Know?
Fundação Nacional do Índio (Funai) is a Brazilian governmental protection agency for Indian interests and their culture.

Many ethnic groups also gather for the Indigenous Peoples' Games to share their cultural traditions and compete in sports events.

Tiradentes Day

April 21 is Tiradentes Day in Brazil. The day commemorates the death of Joaquim José da Silva Xavier, also known as Tiradentes, who was a leading member of a Brazilian **revolutionary** movement. The movement's goal was Brazil's complete independence and freedom from Portugal. When the plan for independence was discovered, Tiradentes was arrested and hanged. Since the 19th century, he has been considered a national hero in Brazil.

Brazil's president and the governor of the state of Minas Gerais attend a ceremony on Tiradentes Day.

Joaquim José da Silva Xavier worked as a dentist before he started the revolutionary movement. Tiradentes Day gets its name from the Portuguese word "tiradentes," which means "tooth-puller." He was given this nickname during a trial following his arrest.

Did You Know?
Many people lay wreaths on the **monument** of Tiradentes in Praça Tiradentes, a plaza named after him.

A number of statues and monuments appear in Brazil to remember Tiradentes and the sacrifice he made for the country.

Labor Day

Another Brazilian national holiday is called Labor Day or International Workers' Day. On May 1 each year, people celebrate the achievements of all workers and the international labor movement in Brazil. There are usually day-long public events, street demonstrations, and marches by working people and their labor unions.

Did You Know?
May 1 is a national holiday in more than 80 countries around the world.

Close to a million people gathered to celebrate Labor Day in Brazil's finanical center in São Paulo on May 1, 2005.

People in Brazil have been celebrating workers on May 1 since 1895, but the day officially became a national holiday in 1925 by a **decree** of President Arthur da Silva Bernardes. On Labor Day, it has become customary for governments to announce the yearly increase in the minimum wage. It is also the day that people's salaries are increased.

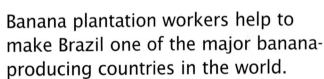

Banana plantation workers help to make Brazil one of the major banana-producing countries in the world.

Feast Days

The feast days of Saint Anthony on June 12, Saint John on June 23, and Saint Peter on June 28 are called Festas Juninas. For two weeks, Brazilians throw outdoor parties with balloons, music, dancing, and barbecued food to celebrate the Festas Juninas and remember and honor these saints.

Did You Know?
Saint Anthony is the patron saint of single men and women. People often stage pretend wedding ceremonies on this feast day.

Festas Juninas celebrations usually take place in an arraial, which is a large building with a **thatched** roof.

Fireworks, bonfires, and religious processions are also often part of the Festas Juninas. In São Paulo, in southern Brazil, people build a huge bonfire that is over 70 feet (21 meters) tall and light it during the Festas Juninas.

Festas Juninas is a country-style party. Men often wear straw hats and women wear their hair in pigtails with painted freckles.

Soldier's Day

People observe Soldier's Day on August 25 each year. On this day, people honor and remember all the soldiers in Brazil and the Brazilian army. This day is also the birthday of a Brazilian war hero named Luís Alves de Lima e Silva, the Duke of Caxias.

A monument in Rio de Janeiro honors the soldiers that died during World War II.

The Duke of Caxias is often recognized as Brazil's greatest military officer.

There is often music and speeches on Soldier's Day. For example, in 2011, the Child Citizen Orchestra was invited to play a special concert for all Brazilian soldiers. The Child Citizen Orchestra is made up of over 100 young people between the ages of three and 17 years old. The children are from the Coque Favela, which is one of the most dangerous neighborhoods in Brazil. They receive free music classes, as well as medical and dental care, food, and uniforms.

Did You Know?
The Brazilian Army fought in several international conflicts in South America during the 19th century, including the Brazilian War of Independence (1822-25).

The Brazilian Army puts their military equipment on display to celebrate Soldier's Day in Brasilia.

Independence Day

September 7 is Independence Day in Brazil. The date commemorates Brazil's declaration of independence from Portugal on September 7, 1822. In Brasilia, the celebration takes place at the Ministries Esplanade with a military parade. Around 30,000 people attend the event each year. Similar military parades are held in many cities throughout the country.

Did You Know?
The president of Brazil attends the Independence Day parade in Brasilia.

On Independence Day, many political leaders appear at public events, including picnics, parades, air shows, and concerts. They talk about Brazil's **heritage**, laws, history, people, and about recent events and future projects. Thousands of Brazilians gather in the streets to celebrate this day. They wave banners, balloons, and streamers. They also proudly fly the Brazilian flag, and sing songs with their friends and families.

The Brazilian Air Force Smoke squadron puts on an air show displaying Brazil's colors on Independence Day in Brasilia.

Our Lady of Aparecida

October 12 is a national holiday in Brazil. This day honors *Nossa Senhora de Aparecida*, or Our Lady of Aparecida, the patron saint of Brazil. On the holiday, about 170,000 people visit the National Sanctuary of Our Lady of Aparecida in Aparecida do Norte, in São Paulo.

The National Sanctuary of Our Lady of Aparecida is one of the most visited places in the entire world.

The National Sanctuary of Our Lady of Aparecida is one of the largest churches in the world. The building is 567 feet (173 meters) long and 551 feet (168 meters) wide. The dome reaches 229 feet (70 meters) and the steeple reaches 334 feet (102 meters).

Approximately 45,000 people can attend Mass at one time at the National Sanctuary of Our Lady of Aparecida.

Did You Know?
A statue of the Virgin Mary represents Our Lady of Aparecida. The statue was caught in the net of three fishermen in October of 1717. Before the statue was caught, they couldn't catch any fish. Afterward, their nets were full.

All Souls' Day

November 2 is All Souls' Day in Brazil. On this national holiday, people honor, remember, and pray for friends and relatives that have died. They visit cemeteries and attend religious services at churches.

Did You Know?
São João Batista in Rio de Janeiro, is one of the most visited cemeteries in Brazil on All Souls' Day. Approximately 800,000 people visit the cemetery during this holiday.

On All Souls' Day people decorate the graves of their deceased relatives with flowers and candles. Some people prepare **altars** in their homes to hold flowers and an offering of food that the deceased enjoyed. Incense, photos, and other reminders of those who have died are often included in the offerings as well.

Many people light candles at the graves of their loved ones in memory of them.

Republic Day

November 15 is Proclamation of the Republic Day in Brazil. Republic Day commemorates the day in 1889 when Brazil's second emperor, Dom Pedro II, was removed from power. Marshal Deodoro da Fonseca declared Brazil a republic on November 15, 1889.

Dom Pedro II **abolished** slavery in 1888. Even though it was a significant achievement, it angered the upper class and contributed to the overthrow of his reign.

There are many events and celebrations throughout the cities and towns of Brazil on Republic Day. For example, in 2011, an organization called *Rodas da Paz*, or Wheels of Peace, celebrated with a bike ride through Brasilia.

Crowds cheer for Marshal Deodoro da Fonseca on November 15, 1889, after Brazil became a republic.

Glossary

abolish To put an end to something; stopping completely

altar A place of worship

decree An order or decision

fast To eat little or no food for a certain amount of time

heritage Something acquired from the past

indigenous Describing the first people living in a certain region

monument Something that serves as a memorial or a place of historic interest

nativity scene A scene showing the baby Jesus in Bethlehem with His mother Mary and His father Joseph

procession A group of people walking in an orderly way

resurrection Rising from the dead

revolutionary Something or someone that brings about big or important changes

thatched A roof made of plant materials such as straw or grass

Index